CW01213184

Original title:
Silver Bells and Silent Nights

Copyright © 2024 Creative Arts Management OÜ
All rights reserved.

Author: Samuel Kensington
ISBN HARDBACK: 978-9916-90-962-1
ISBN PAPERBACK: 978-9916-90-963-8

Luminescence in the Hearth's Glow

The fire crackles, sparks take flight,
My marshmallows burn, oh what a sight!
The cat jumps high, a furry whirlwind,
As I just grin, sweet sugar sinned.

The glow is warm, the jokes come free,
My friends all laugh, it's quite the spree!
The embers dance, a raucous crew,
While my cocoa's gone—what's up with you?

Glittering Pathways of Shadows

The moon crept in, as shadows play,
I tripped on nothing, hip hooray!
A glittering path where no one should roam,
I stumble and mumble, still far from home.

The stars above, like diamonds spill,
I chase them down, against my will!
Each step I take, a comedy show,
With every hop, I shout, 'Oh no!'

Winter's Still Embrace

The snowflakes swirl, like tiny spies,
I lose my balance, oh how I fly!
With frosty boots and scarves galore,
I took a tumble, who could ask for more?

The trees are wrapped in winter's charm,
While I huddle close, to keep me warm.
A snowman stands, all grinned and proud,
With carrot nose, and a scarf so loud!

Moonlit Echoes of Memory

The moon whispers tales of days gone by,
While I forget where I put my pie.
Old friends appear, through the night's cool breeze,
We swap yarns and giggle, and do as we please.

The echoes chime, with laughter vast,
Remembering parties, memories cast.
I'll grab the snacks, oh silly me,
As we moonwalk, quite awkwardly!

The Secret Language of Winter

Winter speaks in icy tones,
With snowflakes dancing on their thrones.
The trees wear coats of frosty white,
While squirrels plot their snowy plight.

Hot cocoa whispers, 'Drink me please!'
As frozen toes beg for some ease.
Snowmen grin with carrot noses,
While kids throw snow like they are roses.

Icicles hang like daggers fine,
A chilly breeze, a glass of wine.
The world is wrapped in quilted dreams,
As winter hums its playful themes.

So bundle up, let laughter ring,
For winter's here with everything.
In every flurry, find the cheer,
For snowball fights are worth a year!

Chilling Whispers in the Still

The winds are sly, the whispers chill,
Invisible folks make mischief, still.
The shadows dance along the ground,
As frosty giggles swirl around.

A cat in boots winks, oh so sly,
While snowflakes tease the naked eye.
Each twig a storyteller's pen,
Crafting tales of what has been.

Mittens lost are sneaky trolls,
And sleigh bells hide as playful souls.
With laughter echoing through the night,
Chilling whispers bring delight.

So grab your scarf, let's make a fuss,
In winter's grasp, we'll find the plus.
With every breeze, a smile we'll fill,
In the laughing night, we find our thrill!

Elysian Nights of Soft Light

The moon's a cookie, round and bright,
Sprinkling crumbs of soft, pale light.
Stars giggle from their sparkling throne,
As night wraps up like a comfy moan.

Each glow of lamp is like a hug,
A warm embrace, a cheerful shrug.
We leap from shadows with a cheer,
Bringing forth the night's grand sphere.

Whispers drift on velvet air,
With secrets shared, beyond compare.
The world is round but feels so flat,
In Elysian light, we chat and chat.

So dance along the starlit way,
In dreams of gold that softly play.
With every step, we lift the night,
In shiny dreams, everything feels right!

Mystic Musing of Short Days

Short days whisper in twilight hues,
As sun dips low, it bids adieu.
We wrap in layers, like a burrito,
And watch as light takes a brisk veto.

The trees wear hats, adorned with fluff,
While shadows stretch, pretending tough.
Each moment's fleeting, yet we smile,
Enjoying the dark, it's worth the while.

Midnight snacks become our quest,
With cookies, chips, we get the best.
The chill invites us in for chat,
A cozy hug, a furry cat.

So here's to nights, both long and bold,
In every story, warmth unfolds.
Embrace the short, for laughter stays,
In mystic musing of our days!

Luminous Shadows in White

In a field of snow I prance,
While my neighbor's dog does dance,
He slips and slides in pure delight,
As I try to catch his flight.

We build a snowman, round and bright,
With a carrot nose, what a sight!
But as the sun begins to glow,
He melts away, oh no, oh no!

The snowballs fly, I hear a shout,
My aim's so good, I knock him out!
But laughter fills the winter air,
As snowflakes tickle without a care.

So here's to winter, crisp and fun,
To winter games and everyone!
We'll dance where shadows shimmer white,
In a world so glowingly bright.

Nocturne of the Whispering Pines

In the forest, secrets hum,
With owls hooting, 'Come, come, come!'
The pines are swaying, what a sight,
As they gossip under moonlight.

Crickets chirp a serenade,
While shadows form a leafy parade.
I trip on roots, oh what a fuss,
The pines just laugh, they don't discuss.

A raccoon steals my trail mix jar,
I chase him under the evening star.
But as I reach, he makes a dash,
And all that's left is a giant splash!

So in the pines, both wise and sly,
Where whispers float and giggles die,
The nocturne plays, oh what a night,
In nature's show, we find delight.

Dreams Wrapped in Glimmer

In the land of dreams, twinkling bright,
I met a star who danced in flight.
He told me tales of wishes grand,
While riding on a comet's band.

A cat in pajamas slept so tight,
While fish played chess by the moonlight.
The clouds were made of marshmallow cream,
As I sipped soda in this dream.

But then the alarm clock rang so loud,
I jumped from bed, I felt so proud.
Yet every night I always find,
The glimmers stay within my mind.

So here's to dreams, both silly and sweet,
Where laughter and wishes joyfully meet,
In glimmering worlds where we still play,
And dance with the stars till break of day.

The Ethereal Dance of Snowflakes

Snowflakes fall like confetti bright,
Each one unique, pure delight.
I catch them on my tongue, so sweet,
As they twirl around my frozen feet.

They whisper secrets, soft and low,
As I spin and twirl in the snow.
A snow angel forms with a flapping sound,
And I giggle at my snowy mound.

The flakes unite for a frosty ball,
Where penguins waddle and snowmen call.
A snowball fight breaks through the cheer,
"Oh watch out! Here comes an icy sphere!"

But as the sun peeks from behind,
The dance slows down, the sun's unkind.
Yet even when they melt away,
The joy they bring will always stay.

Lullabies of the Snowy Vale

In the vale where snowflakes play,
A squirrel skis without delay.
He yells, "Hey! Watch my slide!"
As down the hill he starts to ride.

Snowmen wobble, hats askew,
One snorts, "I'll tell a joke or two!"
They chuckle as their buttons fall,
A snowball fight? They start to brawl!

Frosty winds begin to sing,
Chasing penguins in a ring.
They quack and waddle, what a sight,
Dancing clumsily in the light!

Lullabies of winter's cheer,
With snowflakes giggling, never fear.
As the moon peeks through the trees,
The vale whispers secrets with the freeze.

The Enchantment of Soft Light

In the glow of soft lamp's beam,
A cat yawned, lost in a dream.
He stretched out, oh so profound,
While chasing shadows on the ground.

Two mice played tag on the floor,
While the dog snored, wanting more.
He dreams of tasty treats so fine,
All while the mice dance in line!

The clock chimed once, and twice too,
The room was filled with laughter's hue.
With every tick, the tales run wild,
Where bedtime stories are beguiled.

In the flicker of candle's glow,
Everyone's swaying, taking it slow.
The jokes are silly, the laughter bright,
In this enchantment of soft light.

Frost-Kissed Reverie

A rabbit hopped in boots too big,
He tripped and landed on a twig.
With snowflakes sticking to his nose,
He giggled at his winter clothes.

The trees wore coats of icy sheen,
While squirrels plotted, feeling mean.
They tried to steal a bird's fine seed,
But missed and fell—oh, what a deed!

Icicles dripped like frozen tears,
While penguins waddle, steering clear.
A slip and slide, a joyful scream,
Creating a winter's wacky dream.

Frost-kissed laughs weave through the air,
In this realm of utmost flair.
As snowflakes dance, the world does spin,
In a reverie where joy begins.

Nightfall's Tapestry of Dreams

As the stars twinkle and play,
A raccoon steals the moon's soft ray.
He wraps it in a shiny cloth,
While dreaming of a giant sloth.

The owls hoot a serenade,
While bunnies plot a grand parade.
With carrots decked in ribbons bright,
They hop and skip, such pure delight!

Nightfall blankets the world in grace,
Monkeys swing, an acrobatic race.
They tumble down, a hapless crew,
With giggles and squeals, they are true!

In this tapestry spun so bright,
Whimsy rules the heart of night.
With laughter echoing in the dreams,
A world of joy, or so it seems.

Celestial Carols in the Quiet

Stars hum softly in the night,
While the moon beams with delight.
Snowflakes dance like they're on cue,
Even the owls shout, "Woohoo!"

Comets zip past, oh what a sight,
As space squirrels play with all their might.
Galactic giggles echo far,
Giving the cosmos a friendly spar.

Jupiter's got a jolly grin,
While Saturn spins, just lost in spin.
Uranus laughs with all its rings,
In the silence, joy it brings.

So let's enjoy these celestial tunes,
As they intermingle with joyful moons.
In the quiet, our laughter will soar,
Cosmic carols, forevermore.

Frosty Reveries

Frosty mornings, oh what a tease,
My warm bed's chill, a sweet disease.
Socks on my hands, hat on my face,
Each step outside is a frozen race.

Snowmen plotting as they stand,
"Don't eat the yellow snow," they command!
Icicles hang like giant teeth,
While hot cocoa warms my winter sheath.

Penguins slide and they all cheer,
While I'm just hoping for shoes not to veer.
A gust blows by, chilling my behind,
Who knew winter could be so unkind?

But laughter's warm in snowy lands,
With snowball fights and cold, cold hands.
So let's embrace the frosty dance,
In a winter wonderland, let's take a chance!

Nyctophilia in the Winter

Night falls early, a cozy spree,
Hot chocolate's bubbling, just for me.
Fuzzy blankets wrap me tight,
I'll binge-watch shows in the dim light.

Icicles hang, a sparkly view,
But outside, it's chilly, that much is true.
I'll watch the snowflakes drift and twirl,
While dreaming of summer with a whirl.

The Stillness of Nipped Air

The air's so crisp, it starts to bite,
But my nose thinks it's ready for flight.
Each breath puffs out like a dragon's flame,
Playing outside becomes our game.

Trees wear coats of white and frost,
While I wonder why I feel so tossed.
Hibernation sounds good and wise,
As winter peeks through sleepy eyes.

The stillness sings a chilly tune,
Underneath the watchful moon.
But laughter echoes through the trees,
In this winter magic, feel the breeze.

The Glow of Winter Dreams

Snowflakes dance like clumsy cats,
In pajamas made of fluffy rags.
The icicles hang like crooked smiles,
While squirrels prepare for snack attacks.

Fires crackle, a popcorn treat,
Hot cocoa spills on my new chair.
The snowmen gossip in whispers low,
About snowballs thrown with great flair.

Woolly socks and fuzzy hats,
I trudge through drifts like a big snow beast.
But then I trip and tumble down,
Winter's joy has turned to feast.

So with each slip, I laugh and cheer,
As winter wraps me in its light.
Dreams glow bright, though I might fall,
Bring on the fun, till the spring's in sight!

Midnight's Gentle Serenade

The moonlight sings a silly tune,
While owls hoot in a mellow moon.
Cats strut by with an air so grand,
They think they run the whole night band.

Stars twinkle like they've had too much,
While crickets chirp, a jazzy touch.
Fireflies wink, then disappear,
Illuminating my midnight beer.

A raccoon prances, a knight in trash,
His royal crown, made from a stash.
He tips his hat, gives a sly grin,
As I chuckle, let the show begin!

The clock strikes one, I hear a snore,
Strange sounds echo outside my door.
Midnight's serenade plays on repeat,
Brighten the night with laughter's beat.

Hushed Flakes of Stardust

Hushed flakes drift on a sleepy breeze,
Whispering secrets among the trees.
A rabbit hops in a grand ballet,
Wearing a hat that's stylishly gay.

The frost paints windows with icy art,
While penguins waddle with plenty of heart.
They slide and glide on their snowy stage,
Creating giggles like in a page.

A snowman sports a funky scarf,
While snowflakes giggle and dance with glee.
Each flake a laugh, each flake a jest,
Wrapping winter up in a fluffy vest.

So let the world spin with winter cheer,
With hushed flakes that twinkle near.
In this quiet, giggly embrace,
Joy blankets each chilly space.

Echoes of a Frosted Night

Echoes bounce on the cold, crisp air,
While snowmen plan a midnight fair.
They roll in style, wearing cool shades,
Showing off their frosty charades.

The wind whirls softly, a giggling ghost,
Sausage dogs are what I love most.
With sweater vests, they strut about,
In a canine parade, there's no doubt!

Stars snap photos, click-click-giggle,
As frosty friends make the snow wiggle.
A snowflake sneezes, a mountain's sigh,
A winter night, oh my my my!

We gather 'round, friends made of frost,
In this chill, we'll never feel lost.
Echoes of laughter fill the night air,
Frosted fun beyond compare!

Serenade of the Frosted Pines

The pine trees wear coats, oh so fine,
Where squirrels play tag and toe the line.
A snowman declared it a snowball fight,
With frosty limbs he took to flight.

A snowflake tickled a bear's fuzzy nose,
It turned and sneezed, and off it goes.
The rabbits laughed, in fluffy delight,
As snowballs flew through day and night.

The pines sang loud, in giggles and glee,
While birds brought snacks, oh such a spree.
A blizzard's tune, an icy refrain,
Made snowmen dance across the plain.

So raise your mugs, cheer to the pines,
In the land of frost where laughter shines.
With icy humor and winter's embrace,
We find joy in this frosted place.

Twilight's Breath on Ice

The sun went down in a glittery blaze,
While penguins skated in a curious craze.
They wore tiny hats and twirled with cheer,
As twilight wrapped all in frosty veneer.

An owl hooted, but slipped on the ice,
He flapped and flailed—oh, how not nice!
Bunnies snickered, their noses all pink,
As they sat with tea, making clink-clink.

Then came the stars, with a playful wink,
While shadows danced, making us think.
What secrets lie in the chilly night?
Maybe a snowman with a taste for fright?

So let's raise a glass to the night sky's fun,
To twilight's breath and frosty run.
When laughter echoes on ice so thin,
In this silly world, let the joy begin!

Hallowed Hues of Dusk

Dusk falls softly like a fluffy cat,
While owls debate where they've been at.
The moon peers down with a curious grin,
As shadows play tricks and the giggles begin.

A raccoon stole snacks from under a tree,
He danced with delight as proud as can be.
Squirrels in capes swooped low and high,
As dusk turned the world into a comic pie.

The colors burst in hues quite absurd,
As crickets sang songs that were slightly blurred.
The trees wore hats, the stars wore shoes,
In the hallowed dusk, there's nothing to lose.

So let out a chuckle, and dance with glee,
In the palette of laughter, just let it be.
With dusk's hallowed hues, no worries to find,
In this whimsical world, we wander and unwind.

Shimmering Echoes of Stillness

In the stillness of night, a cat starts to croon,
With glittery stars dancing to the tune.
The mice hold a concert, all dressed in flair,
While owls take selfies, oblivious to a scare.

The moon chuckles softly at their goofy show,
As shadows groove, putting on quite a glow.
A snowflake waltzed with a bundle of cheer,
Swirling and twirling, without any fear.

Then, out of the blue, a gust made it sway,
And off flew the snowflake—a curious ballet!
The trees stood still, but giggles ran free,
In shimmering echoes, we found our glee.

So let's celebrate stillness, with laughter and play,
In the shimmering night where silliness stays.
With echoes that sparkle and dance through the air,
We bubble with joy, without any care.

Twilight's Gentle Whispering

Twilight whispers to the trees,
Silly shadows dance with ease,
A squirrel giggles at the moon,
Says it's time for a raccoon tune.

Fireflies flicker, doing a jig,
While frogs hop around, feeling big,
Crickets tune their late-night song,
Nature's choir, they can't go wrong.

A sleepy owl pretends to yawn,
While an old cat tries to fawn,
Mice gossip about their plans,
To steal some cheese from human hands.

So when twilight starts to creep,
Remember laughs, not just sleep,
For in the dark, joy takes flight,
In the gentle whispers of night.

Beyond the Veil of Frost

Winter's sneezes fill the air,
With frosty flakes in a fluffy hair,
Trees wear coats, oh what a sight,
Not a single branch stays light!

Birds in hats take to the sky,
Wondering how and why they fly,
Snowmen grinning, scarves all nice,
Join the fun, not just in ice!

Hot cocoa flows like lava streams,
With marshmallows dancing like dreams,
While kids in boots make snowballs to throw,
Not knowing how hard they'll glow!

Frosty windows, stories to tell,
Of how joy and ice can dwell,
In a world where cold is king,
Everyone knows laughter's the thing.

Ethereal Glows in the Night's Embrace

Stars twinkle like they stole some bling,
While crickets serenade, trying to sing,
Moonbeams sneak through the creaky door,
Inviting all to the nighttime floor.

Shooting stars race, what a sight!
Don't blink or you'll miss their flight,
Dreamers wish, with hopes held dear,
Just hoping their pizza will appear!

Bats hang out, giving quite the scare,
While dreamy clouds drift without a care,
A glowworm's light flickers so bright,
Making shadows dance with delight!

In this embrace of night so grand,
The world spins gently, hand in hand,
With giggles echoing through the trees,
Underneath the stars, we laugh with ease.

Snowflakes in a Symphony of Silence

Snowflakes waltz, twirling down,
Dressing rooftops in a white gown,
Each one unique, they giggle and sway,
While children cheer, hip-hip-hooray!

Silent nights, a blanket of peace,
Winter's magic feels like a tease,
Snow shovels out their lazy routine,
While penguins slide, oh so serene!

Hot soup bubbles, a steaming pot,
Mittens and hats misplace the plot,
Snowball fights bring squeals of glee,
Who knew winter could be so free?

As the flakes melt, we all know,
The laughter remains, a constant glow,
In every flake that falls from grace,
There's joy in the chilly embrace.

Flickering Candles in Twilight

Flickering candles, oh what a sight,
They dance and sway, just like a fright.
In the corner, a cat in a trance,
Wondering why there's no chance to prance.

Wax drips down like a slow, sad snail,
Lighting up faces, yet making them pale.
"Is it just me, or is it quite hot?"
Said the cake, looking way too distraught.

The shadows giggle, the light plays tricks,
As I bump my head on the candlestick.
A waltz of chaos in my little room,
Where I ponder if candles can dance to a tune.

Oh, flickering candles, you brighten my night,
Making my mishaps a charming delight.
But now I'm off to find a foam hat,
Because the wax is now stuck to my cat!

The Dance of Winter Wishes

Snowflakes twirl, but oh what a jest,
My nose turns pink, it's a chilly fest.
I wished for magic, instead got cold toes,
As frozen fingers wave bye to my nose.

Snowmen wobble, their hats barely stay,
One's falling sideways, what a display!
They raise their carrots in a frosty cheer,
While I close my mouth, holding back a tear.

Slipping and sliding down hills that I crave,
All while avoiding a tumble and wave.
My wish was to glide, now I'm just stuck,
In a snow bank, feeling down on my luck!

Yet laughter erupts as we huddle for warmth,
With hot cocoa dreams on this winter's hearth.
We'll dance around, in our mittens so bright,
Embracing the chill on this magical night!

Memories Wrapped in Warmth

In the attic there's treasure, or so I believe,
Boxes of memories I should not weave.
Old sweaters hug me, two sizes too small,
I once fit in them? I'm no longer tall!

Photo albums that capture the scene,
Of awkward poses and hairstyles obscene.
Laughter erupts from the pages I flip,
It's a cringy journey, oh what a trip!

Popcorn ceilings with stories to tell,
Like that time we thought we could bake a pie well.
It turned to a gooey, exploded display,
Yet memories of chaos warm me today.

Wrapped in a blanket, I giggle with glee,
Those silly old times still bring joy to me.
Memories cherished, all snug by the fire,
They remind me of life, and all I desire!

Moonlit Echoes of Solitude

The moon is a beacon, shining so bright,
Yet here I am, feeling quite the fright.
Staring at shadows, doing the jig,
Wondering if they all think I'm a twig.

Lonely whispers breeze through the trees,
As I debate with my cereal, "Should I sneeze?"
Crickets giggle, and the owls all hoot,
What's wrong with my mind? Why can't I stay mute?

Echoes of laughter from long lost nights,
Chasing away all my silly frights.
Pajamas as armor, I'm ready to fight,
Against the sweet urge to turn off the light.

So, I'll dance with my fears in this moonlit glow,
And waltz with my worries, a delightful show.
Tomorrow I'll wake, so ready to fly,
And leave all this solitude under the sky!

Tales of Cozy Evenings

On a couch that squeaks a little,
I nibble snacks and watch the twiddle.
The cat prefers my warm embrace,
While I delight in clumsy grace.

The TV's on, the popcorn flies,
My drink's a mix of la-la lies.
I snort with laughter, what a sight,
As Batman dances in the night.

The blanket's thrown upon my head,
A cozy fortress for my bed.
I hear the wind begin to howl,
But still I grin, and give a growl.

So here's to nights of silly cheer,
When all our worries disappear.
With hefty snacks and laughter loud,
In cozy evenings, we're all proud.

A Tapestry Woven in White

A tapestry hangs on the wall,
Of snowflakes that seem to gently stall.
Winter's breath kissed all that's bright,
Turning plain gray to pure delight.

In the garden, snowmen grin,
Wearing scarves that I can't begin.
Their carrot noses all askew,
With fluffy hats of icy dew.

With mugs of cocoa, we will cheer,
As we spin tales of yesteryear.
With marshmallows bobbing so light,
In the tapestry woven in white.

So gather 'round, let laughter reign,
As snowflakes dance like joyous rain.
In our cozy nook, as friends unite,
We'll weave dreams through the starry night.

The Softness Beneath Our Feet

There's a magic in the carpet,
Woven fibers that feel like a pet.
Every step's a gentle massage,
Like a thousand marshmallows' collage.

With slippers plush and comfy stance,
I can't resist a silly dance.
The rug's a stage for my grand show,
Where awkward moves steal the whole flow.

Spills and crumbs, oh what a mess,
Yet still, I feel that soft caress.
The floor is calling, "Come and play!"
As I trip over my own sway.

So here's to softness underfoot,
To squishy dreams where laughter's put.
With every step, let silly greet,
The joy of life below our feet.

Echoes in the Violet Veil

In twilight's glow, we share our dreams,
Beneath the stars, where laughter beams.
The violet veil brings tales of cheer,
Echoes of giggles we hold dear.

A bat flies by with a silly screech,
Wings flapping wildly – such an odd breach.
The moon winks down, "Keep it light,"
As shadows dance into the night.

With whispered secrets in the air,
We spin around without a care.
The world is weird, but that's our style,
In echoes wrapped in a violet smile.

So here we are, just you and me,
Dancing 'neath the cosmic spree.
With dreams and giggles on display,
We'll let the night just float away.

Harmonics of Frost and Night

The frost plays a tune on my window pane,
It's like a cold symphony, a chill in the brain.
Squirrels in jackets perform quite a show,
While snowflakes dance lightly, all in a row.

The cats in the moonlight are plotting a scheme,
To steal all the warmth and ruin my dream.
Icicles hang like they're part of a band,
Creating a concert, all snowy and grand.

Chirping of creatures, they sound like a choir,
While snowmen hold meetings, plotting to conspire.
With noses of carrots and smiles so wide,
They're deciding the fate of who gets to slide.

Oh, the harmonics of frost, what a sight to behold,
A whimsical world where chills do not scold.
Just grab your mittens and join in the fun,
For winter's a party that's just begun!

The Calm Before the Snow

The sky wears a blanket of gray and of gloom,
While squirrels prepare for the season of doom.
I brace for the chaos, the lords of the flakes,
As snow plows sharpen their blades for the wakes.

With bread in the oven and hot cocoa too,
I fear the great blizzards may visit anew.
The calm is deceptive, like cats who plot schemes,
They wait for the moment to ruin my dreams.

As winter winds howl like they're plotting a thing,
The snowflakes start falling, their delicate fling.
But I stay indoors with my cozy warm chair,
While outside the chaos creates quite a scare.

Let blizzards blow wildly, let winter winds moan,
I'll sip on my cocoa, I'll safely stay home.
Let snow cover ground like a fluffy white quilt,
In the calm before chaos, I find joy, I'm built!

Enchantment of the Winter Veil

In winter's embrace, the world wears a grin,
Even the grumpy old snowmen wear thin.
The trees don their sparkles, the lights start to brighten,
While critters in sweaters are chasing and bitin'.

The snowflakes are whispers of magic and cheer,
Each one with a tale that we long to hear.
The reindeer are dreaming of biscuits and pies,
While elves play hot poker, oh what a surprise!

Hot cocoa retreats as snowballs engage,
Making brave snowmen feel like they're on stage.
With carrots all crooked for noses so bright,
They practice their pirouettes into the night.

In this enchanting season, who shivers and doubts?
It's all about giggles and sing-a-loud shouts.
So bundle up warmly and join in the dance,
For winter's a party, and we've got a chance!

Whispering Dreams of Distant Shores

The snowflakes are dreaming of faraway lands,
Of beaches with sun and of soft golden sands.
They whisper to each other, "Oh, wouldn't it be,
To trade this cold blanket for warm azure sea?"

Fish in the ocean are jealous for sure,
As penguins in tuxedos start knocking at doors.
They dream of the tropics where sunburns abound,
And flip-flops are worn on the sun-soaked ground.

So let's raise a toast to the wintertime plight,
Where snowmen are singing and stars are so bright.
We'll close our eyes tight and imagine the fun,
As snowflakes keep dancing 'til winter is done.

With whispers of dreams from those distant shores,
We'll relish the magic that winter restores.
So gather your mittens and don your best cheer,
For every snowstorm brings joy, my dear!

The Gentle Lull of Dark Mornings

The rooster's lost its voice, it seems,
He'd rather play in dreamland's beams.
The sun is snoozing, oh what a sight,
While coffee calls, 'I'm here! Delight!'

The cat's furball symphony begins,
As socks find their way to chinchilla wins.
The warmth of blankets hugs us tight,
In morning's chill, we shun the light.

The toast pops up like a happy clown,
While butter slides right down and frowns.
The gentle lull of morning's tease,
Turns sleepy grunts into soft wheeze.

So let us laugh as darkness fades,
With sleepy smiles, our dreams cascades.
In the gentle glow of coffee's charm,
We face the world, not a hint of harm.

A Melody in Frosted Breaths

Frosty whispers dance in air,
As noses freeze in morning's flair.
Chattering teeth, a merry song,
The gloves are lost, what came wrong?

Snowflakes flutter like tiny spies,
Sneaking peeks from winter's skies.
The scarf's a ninja, wrapped too tight,
Turning giggles into frosty fright.

A rabbit hops by with curious style,
While icicles hang with a frozen smile.
A snowman winks with a carrot nose,
While passersby slip in frosty clothes.

As children laugh and tumble around,
In winter's charm, such joy is found.
A melody in frosted breaths,
Wraps us all in frosty hefts.

The Radiance of Cold Dreams

Cold dreams twinkle like stars on ice,
While penguins in tuxedos think they're nice.
With flippers flapping, they waddle and slip,
Who needs a boat with such a cool trip?

Hot chocolate spills, an avalanche rise,
As marshmallows float like fluffy skies.
The snowflakes giggle, a soft ballet,
While snowmen plot their snowy play.

The moon's a giant cookie on high,
While shadows muse and lullabies sigh.
The radiance of dreams, cheeky and bright,
Keeps us grinning through the cold night.

So snuggle tight, with blankets galore,
In dreams of winter, we always explore.
A quilt of laughter, our cozy theme,
Wrapped in the warmth of our cold dreams.

Shimmers Through the Frosty Pines

Frosty pines wear coats of white,
While squirrels plan their morning flight.
The pine cones whisper secrets old,
While winter tales of magic unfold.

Beneath the branches, giggles abound,
As snowballs fly in a snowy round.
The grumpy owl just shakes his head,
While young ones laugh, no time for bed.

The sun peeks in with golden rays,
Turning the frost into sparkly plays.
Shimmers through the frosty pines,
A winter wonder where joy aligns.

So build a fort and ride a sleigh,
In this chilly but merry ballet.
With hearts aglow, let spirits climb,
Through laughter and smiles, our best winter time.

Hushed Tones of the Chilly Eve

The moon whispers secrets, oh what a sight,
A penguin in pajamas says, "It's too bright!"
Snowflakes are dancing, all glued to my nose,
I'm shivering mostly in places, who knows?

A snowman is plotting to steal my hot drink,
His carrot is winking, it makes me rethink.
With mittens so fluffy, I slip and I slide,
This frosty adventure, I'll bumble with pride!

The wind sings a tune, it's awkward and weird,
Like a cat stuck in a tree, quite confused and smeared.
The chilly eve giggles, I trip on a sleigh,
Laughing at my joy, in its own icy way.

Oh winter, you jester, with snow on your chin,
You tickle my toes and give cold feats a spin.
Let's toss snowballs, and giggle till dawn,
For tomorrow I'll snooze like a frozen sweet fawn.

Glistening Secrets of an Icy Night

Stars in the sky with a twinkle of glee,
They're plotting a heist, come witness with me!
The snowman's got plans, oh dear, what a fright,
He's arming his army with glittering light.

The trees are all draped in a sparkling cloak,
As if they were dressed by a well-versed bloke.
Icicles dangled like swords of the night,
Beware of the frost, it's a slippery bite!

Fairies with mittens are busting a move,
They tango on rooftops, oh what a groove!
But wait till they slip, and oh, what a crash,
They'll giggle and rise with a bright, snowy splash.

In this glittery chaos, I roll with delight,
Slipping and laughing, oh what a night!
With glistening secrets and childish glee,
Who knew icy mischief could be so carefree?

Celestial Lullabies in the Quietude

The stars hum a tune, like a cat's gentle purr,
As I lay in the snow, feeling slightly demure.
The moon's got a giggle, it beams with a grin,
"Can I borrow your blanket? It's chilly, come in!"

The cosmos is wrapping me snug with its light,
Whispering lullabies through the crisp, cheerful night.
"Dream of chocolate rivers or bikes made of cheese,
Where snowmen wear hats and frolic with ease!"

A comet zooms past, in a jolly whirl,
As I chuckle at space, under its fantastic twirl.
The clouds are like marshmallows, soft and so sweet,
While penguins in slippers have come for a treat!

With each twinkle above, my worries take flight,
In celestial dreams, everything's just right.
Hushed tones of the evening wrap me like a hug,
In this wintry wonder, I'm snug as a bug.

The Sparkle of Distant Dreams

In the distance, I hear a delightful banter,
The twinkling stars playgames with a phantom dancer.
"Do you think they can see us?" a snowflake asks wide,
"Or do they just gossip from that cosmic slide?"

A comet rolls by, wearing sunglasses galore,
While asteroids clap, begging for more.
The cosmos all chuckles, with sparkles of fun,
As my dreams take flight like a plane on the run.

The moon makes a smoothie to share with the night,
While the sun brushes dust with a dreamy delight.
The sparkle of dreams, oh what a wild quest,
Every wink of the stars feels like being blessed!

With laughter and joy, every shadow ignites,
In this whimsical galaxy, everything excites.
Distant dreams shimmer, as wild as can be,
Come join my adventure, and together you'll see!

Notes from an Icy Silence

Whispers of snow, a chilly hush,
Squirrels in coats, all in a rush.
Snowflakes prance, they don't look shy,
As penguins slide—oh my, oh my!

Hot cocoa steams in mugs so bright,
Marshmallows dance in creamy delight.
Fingers numb, yet spirits soar,
What's next? A snowball fight galore!

Frosty windows show a world so still,
I wish my socks could feel this thrill.
But here I sit, wrapped up like toast,
Surveying my ice-capped, chilly coast.

Yet from the quiet, a giggle breaks,
As snowmen tumble in funny fakes.
Who knew icy silence could yield such fun?
In the land of cold, comedy's just begun!

Scarves and Softness Under Stars

Wrapped in layers, a fashion crime,
Scarves all knotted—oh, what a time!
Fuzzy hats with pom-poms high,
Look like mushrooms! I can't deny.

Under the stars, we chase a dream,
While sipping cocoa, or so it seems.
Frozen noses, cheeks like roses,
I swear these cold nights have funny poses.

Laughter bounces off icicles bright,
As we trip over our coats in the night.
Softness abounds, though senses freeze,
In this winter wonderland, joy's the tease!

So here we are, all snug and tight,
Wishing for warmth in the frosty night.
Who needs a heater, or a fire's glow?
When laughter's warmth makes our hearts grow!

The Silken Touch of Winter Air

Winter's breath, a frosty kiss,
Is it cold, or pure abyss?
The trees wear white, a fancy dress,
While penguins wobble—what a mess!

Skating on ice, all graceful like,
Until I slip and take a hike!
Giggles follow with every fall,
As snowballs fly and laughter calls.

The air so crisp, a biting joy,
Feeling like a clumsy toy.
Yet magic dances in every breath,
As we build snow forts, defy our death.

Frosty whispers in the night,
Wrap up warm, hold on tight!
Come join the fun in winter's chill,
Where laughter echoes, and hearts will thrill!

A Gallery of Frosted Wishes

Frosted wishes hung on trees,
A gallery that swings with ease.
While snowflakes giggle as they fall,
And snowmen stand, quite proud and tall.

We scribble dreams on icy panes,
Hot chocolate guards against the gains.
While mittened hands wave to the stars,
With hopes as bright as candy bars.

In this frosty gallery of cheer,
Every twinkle brings good cheer.
With snowball fights and snowy trails,
We chase our joy with winter's gales.

So hang your wishes, let them shine,
In this icy world, all is divine.
For laughter's warmth will always stay,
In frosted dreams, come laugh and play!

Frosted Dreams Beneath the Stars

In winter's chill, we dream of warmth,
Hot cocoa mugs, our hearts they swathe.
With marshmallows floating, sweet delight,
We toast to snowmen, what a sight!

Frosted windows paint the scene,
A snowball fight—oh, how we gleam!
With laughter echoing through the night,
I can't believe I lost that fight!

Under stars that twinkle bright,
We dance around, with all our might.
Slipping, sliding on icy lanes,
Oh, winter's joy, it never wanes!

So gather round, let's sing a song,
Of frosted dreams where we belong.
With friends and fun and winter cheer,
Our hearts are light, we have no fear!

The Serenade of Winter's Call

A snowflake lands upon my nose,
It tickles me, and then it froze.
I sneeze and snort, like some old bear,
My frosty breath fills up the air!

The wind it howls, a wild refrain,
Like cats in choir, driving me insane.
Yet with each gust that whips and swirls,
I laugh aloud, let laughter unfurl!

The world is wrapped in crisp white sheets,
But in my heart, the warmth still beats.
I pull on socks in mismatched pairs,
And dance like no one ever cares!

Oh winter, you are quite a tease,
With every chill, there's joy with ease.
So sing along to winter's grace,
And wear that silly hat in place!

Unveiling the Quiet Beauty

The trees stand tall, their branches bare,
A quiet beauty fills the air.
I stumble 'round in snowdrift dreams,
With frigid thoughts and wobbly schemes.

The world is muted, hush-hush, hush!
But here I am, a clumsy crush.
I trip on ice, my dignity lost,
Yet find the joy amidst the frost!

In quiet moments, laughter bursts,
As neighbors slip in frosty bursts.
With giggles shared in winter's dance,
We find our joy in every chance.

So let us freeze but not freeze up,
With stories shared from a hot cup.
Embrace the quiet winter glow,
And laugh at what we cannot know!

Embraces of the Long Night

The nights are long, the candles burn,
Snuggled up, it's my turn.
With blankets piled up high and tight,
I binge on shows till morning light.

The cat's afoot on twisty feet,
He claims my lap as his warm seat.
With purring loud and snores galore,
I can't help but chuckle and implore!

Outside the world is frosty-fine,
But here inside, everything's divine.
With cookies baked and cocoa hot,
What better joy? I think not!

So here's to nights that never end,
To cozy vibes we all commend.
In winter's grip, we find delight,
In embraces through the chilly night!

Illuminated Paths in a Chilled Silence

On a frosty night I tripped,
While the moonlight slyly sipped.
My nose turned red like a cherry,
As I skated, oh so merry.

Snowflakes danced, a waltz so grand,
I slipped and fell, they took my hand.
But every tumble brought a grin,
I found the joy beneath the skin.

Laughter echoed through the trees,
I lost my hat to a cheeky breeze.
The path was lit, but also slick,
I made a snow angel, that's my trick.

With friends like these, who needs a map?
We sled down hills, what a crazy lap.
In chilled silence, hilarity reigns,
As we share our giggles and our pains.

Tranquil Reflections on Icy Waters

By the lake, a mirror bold,
Where fish have tales that must be told.
I tried to fish, but caught a shoe,
The water laughed, it knew what to do.

The ducks quacked in a perfect line,
One lost his way, said, "That's just fine!"
He wobbled left and then the right,
Even ducks have a silly sight.

Icebergs float like frozen dreams,
While chilly whispers turn to screams.
My hot cocoa spilled, oh what a sight,
As I slipped and took flight into the night.

Though tranquil waters tried to tease,
With laughs and spills, they aimed to please.
Reflections gleamed with laughter's grace,
We skated on smiles, what a crazy place!

Luminescence Beneath the Midnight Sky

Stars twinkled like a giant's bling,
I danced beneath, let my heart sing.
Then I stumbled on a snow mound,
And heard the world's laughter resound.

The northern lights put on a show,
But my mom's casserole stole the glow.
I yelled, "What's that? A dancing light!"
Oh wait, it's just my neighbor's kite.

With each move, I turned a twist,
Fell in a snowbank, not to be missed.
The midnight air with jokes so airy,
No better time to be quite merry.

Beneath the sky, we laughed aloud,
In this winter's wonder, we're so proud.
With every tumble, every cheer,
We brightened up this frosty sphere.

The Hush of a Winter's Tale

In the hush of snow, a tale unfolds,
Of frozen mishaps and icebergs bold.
With every step, I brought a thud,
As I made a splash in the puddly mud.

A squirrel peeped to share my feud,
His acorn stash was just my food.
We eyed each other, approval so near,
With snacks exchanged, we conquered fear.

In winter's tales, we knit our fates,
A hot chocolate banter as friendship waits.
Through frosty whispers, laughter rings,
'Tis the joy that winter brings!

So with cheeks rosy, and hearts so bright,
In the hush of the snow, our spirits take flight.
A tale to cherish, quite unique,
In every giggle, winter would speak.

Soft Tones of a Forgotten Song

In an attic, a cat plays a tune,
With a banjo, and a fading moon.
The notes are wobbly, a bit off-key,
Even the mice are laughing with glee.

A ghost joins in, full of sass,
Dancing on tables, making a fuss.
Together they jam, with joy and cheer,
While the dust bunnies roll in, clutching a beer.

The old record spins, then skids and stops,
As the cat gives a grin, and the ghost hops.
It's a party of sorts, in this old, dim light,
But the only ones here are feline and fright.

So if you hear music on a quiet night,
Don't check the radio; it's quite a sight!
Just a cat in an attic, with a ghost by its side,
Soft tones of a song where the fun is a ride.

Moonlit Reveries in the Frosty Air.

The moon hangs low, like a pizza pie,
I swear it winked at me as it passed by.
Chilled air nips at me, it's biting and bold,
My cheeks turn red like the stories of old.

I stomp through the snow, just to hear the crunch,
But it echoes back, 'Did you skip lunch?'
Frozen faces in windows all giggle and tease,
Their laugh is contagious, it makes me freeze.

An owl hoots loudly, I give him a glare,
Is it too late to ask if he wants a chair?
But he just keeps hooting, like he knows the score,
"Got no time for humans; there's wisdom galore!"

So I shuffle away, with a grin on my face,
Under the moon's light, I quicken my pace.
For who needs wisdom when the stars play along,
In moonlit reveries, I'm singing a song.

Whispers of Frosty Evenings

Frosty evenings, when the world takes a breath,
The trees are like ice, as if frozen to death.
"My branches are cold!" the old oak does groan,
While squirrels gather acorns for supper alone.

The wind whistles through, like a bad singer's tune,
It rattles the shutters, and shimmies the moon.
"Keep it down, will ya?" the moon starts to pout,
As whispers of frost begin to freak him out.

A rabbit hops by, in a scarf made of cheese,
"Why are you staring, oh wintery freeze?
Just minding my business, no need for a show,
I'd trade you a carrot for warmth, you know!"

But frost only chuckles, with a shivery grin,
"Let's dance all night, let the chill begin!"
And under the stars, they all twirl and spin,
In whispers of frosty evenings, laughter wins.

Chimes Beneath the Moonlight

Beneath the moonlight, the wind chimes swing,
They clank and they clatter; oh what a thing!
A melody born of mischief and cheer,
"Or was it the cat?" I might need a beer.

Ghosts join the chorus, with spirits so bright,
They dance with the shadows, a comical sight.
"Play us a tune!" they chant with delight,
So I grab my spoons, and join them tonight.

The neighbor's dog barks, "What's all this fuss?"
"Just some moonlit magic; no need to make a fuss!"
With a wag of his tail, he joins in the fun,
And we all laugh together, 'til the night's all but done.

So if you hear chimes under stars shining bright,
Just know it's a party, every soft night.
With laughter and music, the world feels just right,
In chimes beneath moonlight, we take flight.

The Lightness of Eerie Sighs

In the dark when shadows loom,
I heard a sigh, and things went boom.
Was it a ghost or just my snack?
Either way, I'm not going back!

The wind it whispers, secret tales,
Of flying cats and fish with scales.
I chuckle loud, then shiver some,
Just hope they don't think I'm too dumb.

A candle flickers, tales unspool,
A poltergeist in my old school.
"Hey!", I shout, "Is that you, Dave?"
But silence answers; I feel brave.

Yet still I wonder, late at night,
Who else is here in ghostly fright?
With lightness odd and eerie sighs,
I drift to sleep, under dark skies.

Glacial Glow in the Quietude

Snowflakes twirl like dancers, bold,
Each one a story, secrets told.
They chill my nose, they freeze my toes,
I laugh, 'cause winter always knows.

The moonlight casts a frosty glow,
Where snowmen grinning start to grow.
Their carrot noses look quite chic,
But watch out, they might just squeak!

I sled down hills on bits of plastic,
'Til I crash into a tree, fantastic!
The forest whispers, "Let's start again,"
"Just watch out for that old, grumpy hen!"

In glacial glow, we dance and spin,
With frozen fingers, let fun begin.
Amidst the chill, we find our muse,
In this winter wonderland, we choose.

Serenity Wrapped in White

The world adorned in winter's veil,
Where snowflakes fall without fail.
Trees stand silent, wrapped up tight,
Like marshmallows in a snowy fight.

I did a flip, thought I'd impress,
But ended up in winter's mess.
Flapping arms like fluffy wings,
I can't believe the joy it brings!

The air is crisp, as dogs do prance,
Chasing shadows, they take a chance.
While humans slip and land so nice,
It's pure comedy, not once, but twice!

Serenity fills the frozen air,
With laughs and giggles everywhere.
Wrapped in white, we find delight,
In this snowy world, oh what a sight!

Poetry of the Wintered Wind

The winter wind sighs soft and low,
A chilly bard with tales to throw.
I grab my hat, and snug it tight,
For poetry comes deep in the night.

The trees they dance, creak and sway,
In rhythmic beats, they join the play.
"Who needs a band?" I wonder aloud,
With nature's tunes, I'm feeling proud.

A snowman's nose just took a dive,
With every puff, it stays alive.
His smile wide, a frosty grin,
"Hey buddy, let the fun begin!"

So here I sit with pen in hand,
Writing verses of this snowy land.
In the wintered wind, my thoughts unwind,
A poetry dance—oh, it's divine!

Soft Echoes Beneath the Snow

Snowflakes dance on the ground,
As squirrels make tiny sounds.
A snowman struts with a carrot nose,
He tells the trees all his jokes, I suppose.

Snow boots slip on a patch of ice,
Falling over is not very nice.
A penguin slides by, wearing a hat,
He quips, "You humans, now that's where it's at!"

Frozen tongues stuck to poles,
Kids in mittens, playing roles.
Hot cocoa spills, what a delight,
Laughter echoes through the night.

Yet beneath all the snow's cool flair,
A brave little worm finds a warm chair.
He giggles softly, not a care,
"As long as it's winter, I'll be here to share!"

Reflections of a Shimmering Comet

A comet zooms, oh what a sight,
With a tail so long, it sparks delight.
Aliens wave from their glowing ship,
While Martians say, "Please don't let it slip!"

Asteroids dodge in a cosmic race,
While Jupiter gives a friendly face.
Venus blushes, she's quite shy,
While Saturn's rings spin on high.

Earthlings at night point with glee,
"Look at that star, it's so free!"
Little do they know up above,
There's a celestial dance of alien love.

With every flash, and every swoosh,
The universe hears the comets' whoosh.
They whisper secrets so grand and loud,
That even the farthest black hole is proud!

Frosted Dreams in the Moonlit Quiet

The moonlight glimmers on frosty grass,
Where bunnies prance and clovers pass.
A snowman dreams of summer's heat,
While icicles tap a chilly beat.

Stars twinkle like childhood wishes,
While snowflakes perform their circle swishes.
A wise old owl hoots with flair,
"Can you hear the sound of free air?"

Glistening dreams ride on winter's breeze,
While penguins waddle with such ease.
Frosty critters in cozy beds,
Telling tales in their fluffy heads.

So here's to dreams all frosty and bright,
Under the glow of the soft moonlight.
Where laughter sparkles all around,
And fun in frosted dreams is found!

Muffled Footsteps on a Starlit Path

Starlit paths beneath our feet,
With giggles that make the night sweet.
Footsteps shuffle, then suddenly pause,
As a raccoon struts with a little applause.

Toadstools glowing, mushrooms wink,
While fireflies dance, and owls blink.
Every shadow holds a surprise,
As the night whispers through the skies.

Midnight snacks in a forest nook,
Pairing snacks with a good storybook.
"Who ate the last cookie?" a voice calls,
As a curious fox near the tree falls.

So wander here where laughter's the song,
On a starlit path where we all belong.
With frolicking fun under the moon,
The night says, "Stay out a little more, soon!"

Milton Keynes UK
Ingram Content Group UK Ltd.
UKHW022102091224
452221UK00007B/80